My First Book About the Birds of North America

I0422909

Amazing Animal Books

Children's Picture Books

By Molly Davidson

Mendon Cottage Books

JD-Biz Publishing

Download Free Books!

http://MendonCottageBooks.com

All Rights Reserved.

No part of this publication may be reproduced in any form or by any means, including scanning, photocopying, or otherwise without prior written permission from JD-Biz Corp and http://AmazingAnimalBooks.com. Copyright © 2015

All Images Licensed by Fotolia, Pixabay, and 123RF

Read More Amazing Animal Books

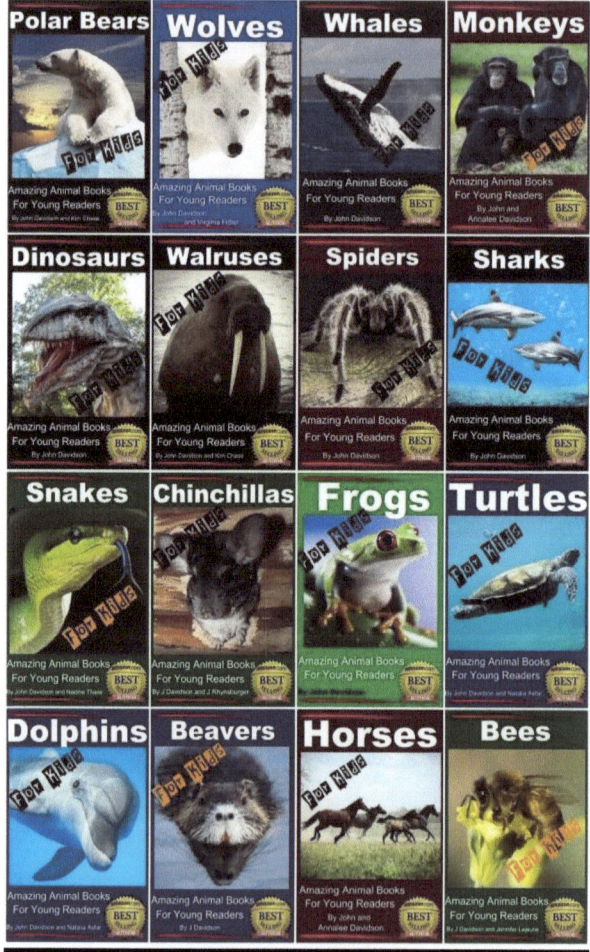

Purchase at Amazon.com

Table of Contents

Introduction...5

 Common North American Bird Families 5

Knowing More about the Birds around You – Fun Facts of the More Common Bird Species 8

All About Blackbirds...8

Amazing Sparrow Facts...11

Amazing Facts and Information About Hawks......13

Facts about the Cranes 16

Facts about the Goldfinch.......................................19

Facts and Information about Ducks........................21

Facts and Information on Bluc Jays 23

Facts and Information on Chickadees 25

Facts and Information on Egrets.............................26

Facts and information about Vultures 28

Fun Facts About Falcons 31

Fun Facts and Information about Gulls..................35

Information and Facts About Finches 38

Interesting Facts and Information about Owls 40

Some Basic Facts and Information about Doves....44

Some information on Orioles (the bird, not the baseball team) 46

Learning Facts and information about Sandpipers.48

Learn All About Eagles 50

    Bald Eagles 52

Why Everyone's Kingfisher Is Different 56

Useful Facts and Information on Woodpeckers 57

Information on Roadrunners....................................60

Canadian Geese...63

Top Facts and Information about Flycatchers........65

The Ins and Outs of Warblers 68

Information and Facts about the American Robin .71

Conclusion 74

Publisher 81

Introduction

Common North American Bird Families

North America is home to a number of bird species and families, here are a few:

Anatidae is one common North American bird family. This group includes geese, swans, and ducks.

Strigidae is another common type of North American bird; we usually hear it called an owl.

Another popular North American bird family is the **Columbidae**, which are pigeons and doves.

The penguin belongs to the **Spheniscidae** family, another common North American bird.

Pelecanidae is a popular bird family; this family has herons, egrets, and birds that wad in the swaps.

The **Phoenicopteridae** family also lives in North America. These birds can stand as tall as 5 feet, they are called flamingos.

Knowing More about the Birds around You – Fun Facts of the More Common Bird Species

All About Blackbirds

A boy blackbird

Blackbirds got their name because they really are a bird that is the color black.

They are NOT crows or ravens, who are also black.

Blackbirds are quick to attack. If they feel like they are in danger, they will run around dipping their head up and down.

If the intruder still attacks, it is usually a short fight; the blackbird wins most of the time.

Blackbirds eat earthworms, berries, seeds, and many kinds of insects.

The number of blackbirds is very high. They are healthy and continuing to have new baby blackbirds.

Amazing Sparrow Facts

A boy sparrow

Sparrows can live just about anywhere. Any continent, in a warehouse, they have even been found in underground coal mines.

House sparrows eat seeds and plants, but in the springtime they can be found gathering insects.

Sparrow babies, called chicks, must be ready to fly from the nest within two weeks of hatching.

Sparrows like to build their nets in people buildings, they are protected, and usually there is human garbage around, which is an easy food source.

Some people even build bird houses for sparrows to eat from.

Amazing Facts and Information About Hawks

Red Tailed Hawk in flight

Hawks are part of the same bird family as vultures, ospreys, and falcons.

Girl hawks are stronger and larger than the boys.

They are able to capture their prey, and tear it apart, using their very sharp curved beaks and talons (claws).

Hawks have very good eyes. They can fly high above their prey, and then pounce on them from above.

An owl hawk

Hawks hunt during the day, for smaller birds and some smaller animals, like rabbits, snakes, squirrels, and mice.

Like most birds, hawks have oil that naturally covers their feathers, making them waterproof and helping them to fly.

When they build a nest, they will build in trees, or on rocky cliffs to keep their babies safe from harm.

Facts about the Cranes

Sandhill Cranes

This large bird is found on everywhere except in South America and in Antarctica.

The Japanese consider the crane to be a National Treasure.

The Sandhill crane is the most common crane in the world.

The Sandhill crane will eat whatever is available, including tubers, worms, and even snakes.

Whooping cranes can be as tall as 5 feet.

Whooping cranes eat lots of blue crabs before they migrate to Texas, Florida, and Louisiana for the winter.

A whooping crane

Fossils have proven that cranes have been on this Earth for about 10 million years.

Facts about the Goldfinch

The Goldfinch is a small bird about 5 inches in length.

They eat seeds, berries, and grains.

They are easy to spot, because they have a bright lemon yellow body, white under tail, and black wings.

The goldfinch lives along country roads and in fields.

Many goldfinches will build their nests in the same place year after year.

Facts and Information about Ducks

Ducks can live in saltwater and fresh water.

They eat fish, grass, worms, insects, and some tree leaves.

Muscovy ducks

Ducks weigh about 7 - 9 pounds.

Boy ducks are called Drakes, the girl ducks are called Ducks, and the babies are called ducklings.

A duck wings are short and pointed, which helps them fly for a long or a short distance.

Facts and Information on Blue Jays

Winter Blue Jay

Blue Jays can copy the sounds of other birds.

Blue Jays are known for stealing eggs from other birds' nests!

They eat acorns, nuts, seeds, grasshoppers, caterpillars, and beetles.

Blue Jays will sometimes migrate south for the winter, and others times they will not. Scientists do not know why they don't always migrate.

Facts and Information on Chickadees

Black-capped Chickadees on a branch

Chickadees nest in trees, bushes, and some will even steal an old woodpeckers' nest for their own. Also they may nest in a hole in the ground or in rock.

They love to eat seeds, especially sunflower seeds. Chickadees also eat spiders, spider larvae, and nuts.

Facts and Information on Egrets

Egrets live in wetlands and swamps, mostly in North and South Carolina.

Great White Egret

They build their nests in trees and gather with other wetland birds in groups.

Egrets are part of the Heron family of birds.

Great Blue Heron

Egrets eat fish, which they grab quickly out of the water with their long sharp bills.

Facts and information about Vultures

Endangered California condor flying

Condor is another name for vulture.

They like to scavenge, which means steal food some other animal has already been killed or an animal that has died, for their food, instead of hunting it themselves.

They will eat everything on a dead animal, only leaving behind the bones.

Griffon Vulture

They are found many places on Earth except for Antarctica and Australia.

Vultures like to stay by themselves; they don't normally hang out in groups.

Fun Facts About Falcons

A falcon perched on its trainers hand

Falcons get confused with hawks; their bills are notched instead of smooth like hawks.

Falcons have long and pointed wings built for speed and moving well in the air.

Gyrfalcons are the largest of the falcons, and only kings could use them for hunting.

Gyrfalcon

Gyrfalcons are able to live, hunt, and even lay their eggs in Arctic regions.

The peregrine falcon has been recorded flying at more than 200 miles per hour, when diving for prey.

A Peregrine Falcon perched on a stump

Peregrine Falcons have been seen flying around skyscrapers, in big cities, hunting pigeons.

The Merlin falcon was used and trained by women in Europe, for hunting.

Merlin Falcon

They can patrol big meadows and shorelines for their prey, which is smaller birds and dragonflies.

Falcons are amazing hunters and have been used by humans to hunt for hundreds of years.

Fun Facts and Information about Gulls

Herring Gull

One of the most noisiest of all birds is the seagull.

They can drink saltwater and fresh water, not many birds can do that.

Gulls mostly live by the coast.

They eat fish, shell fish, grubs, grasshoppers, and earthworms.

A mother and father gull will take turns sitting on their egg, until it hatches.

They save energy by gliding in the air, and they soak up heat from the paved roads in the winter, keeping them warmer.

Lastly, seagulls are the state bird of Utah.

Information and Facts About Finches

Zebra Finches

Many people would rather have a finch as a pet than a parrot or a parakeet.

Finches need other finches, so if you have a pet finch, you will need more than one.

Finches do not like to be touched; they prefer to just be left to fly around.

These birds only weigh less than one ounce (the weight of a marble) and are less than 4 inches long!

Since finches are so small, they also have tiny voices, they sing and chirp a lot, but they are heard very softly in the background.

Interesting Facts and Information about Owls

Owls cannot move their eyes; this is why they can turn their heads almost all the way around.

A Great Horned Owl

Owls like to hunt for food at night.

Owls eat fish, mice, insects, and small rodents.

A Barn Owl

Owls have heavier wings; this is helpful, because when they fly, they are silent.

Owls, like all other birds, have no teeth with which to eat or chew their prey. They swallow their prey whole.

A Great Gray Owl

A group of owls is called a parliament.

Owls are many different colors; most owls are the same color as where they live. This way they can stay safe by being camouflaged.

A baby owl, called an owlet

Some Basic Facts and Information about Doves

Doves live in towns and cities, they don't like the woods.

They use telephone wires as a perch.

Doves have a familiar cooing sound; they make the "who-who-who" call.

Doves that live in cities and towns live about 11 years.

Doves are quick fliers. They use their tails to make steep dives and to steer them while flying.

Some information on Orioles (the bird, not the baseball team)

A girl Baltimore Oriole bird

Orioles lives mainly along the east or Atlantic coast of the United States.

Orioles migrate to the south, for warmer weather, in the winter.

Orioles build hanging nests on the end of tree branches.

The mother and father oriole will raise the babies.

Learning Facts and information about Sandpipers

Least sandpiper

The sandpiper is a bird that usually floats or wades by the shore of oceans.

Sandpipers are found all over the world in different climates, and they usually hang around the water.

They also have shorter bills than other birds, and chirp more when they are flying, rather than when they are on the ground or in the water.

Learn All About Eagles

There are two types of eagles in Canada and the Unites States, the Golden Eagle and the Bald Eagle.

Golden Eagle

The eagle is second biggest bird; the biggest is vultures.

Eagles have long, hooked beaks, making it easier for them to tear apart their prey.

Bald Eagles like to grab fish out of rivers and streams.

Eagles have such power and strength; they are usually at the top of the food chain.

Bald Eagles

In 1967, the bald eagle was put on the endangered species list, but in 2007, after 40 years, the population had grown so it was taken off.

The American bald eagle is the national birth of North America.

Eagles live about 15 - 20 years.

The bald eagle it is not bald at all! The word bald actually means white, and it has a white head.

Their beak is sharp, at the tip it has a hook which is used for tearing flesh of their prey and it can also be used as a weapon.

Half of the bald eagles in the world live in Alaska and in British Columbia, Canada.

An eagle's vision is four times better than a human with perfect vision.

Eagles have a high pitched cry, but they don't have any vocal cords, they make the sound using a bony chamber which vibrates.

Why Everyone's Kingfisher Is Different

The kingfisher family of birds lives all over the World. Except they do not like the Arctic or very dry deserts.

Most of these birds live near water and eat fish.

Kingfishers live in dirt holes, rather than a nest.

Useful Facts and Information on Woodpeckers

A boy Pileated Woodpecker on a dead pine tree

A pileated woodpecker is the largest woodpecker; it is the size of a crow!

Woodpeckers have a red strip that starts at the crown (top) of their head, and runs all the way down their neck.

Great Spotted Woodpecker

They eat insects, acorns, berries, nuts, and tree sap.

Woodpeckers have a large hammering head, with a sharp straight beak. This is used for hammering holes in trees.

Red Headed Woodpecker

Information on Roadrunners

Roadrunners can fly, but most of the time they are running on the ground, at about 20 miles per hour.

Roadrunners mostly eat worms and insects; sometimes they will eat crickets, lizards, snakes, scorpions, bird eggs, and even hummingbirds.

They have one toe in the front of their foot, and two in the back.

These birds live in the desert areas of the United States.

To get rid of extra salt in their bodies, roadrunners have a gland in front of its eyes that will push out the salt.

Canadian Geese

Canadian Geese live in the colder areas of North America.

The Canadian Goose has a unique white band, called a chinstrap, under it face.

The boys and girls look basically the same; the difference is in their voices.

They migrate in the winter to California, South Carolina, and Mexico.

Top Facts and Information about Flycatchers

Willow flycatcher perched on a tree branch

They can actually grow over a foot in length, and will often nest in bushes or trees.

Flycatchers eat dragonflies, grasshoppers, and robber flies.

A girl Hill Blue Flycatcher

They catch their food like a hawk; they fly high then dive down on their prey.

These birds are found in Northern and Central America; usually in an evergreen forest.

Black Phoebe Flycatcher

The Ins and Outs of Warblers

Black-Throated Blue Warblers

Boy warblers are bright blue and girl warblers are a duller color.

Warblers live all over North America, but their favorite places are Virginia and Missouri.

Warblers eat mostly insects.

Northern Parula Warbler

In the winter, warblers migrate to South America, where it is much warmer.

A girl Yellow Rumped Warbler

Warblers lay 3 - 4 eggs anytime in April or May.

Information and Facts about the American Robin

Robins live in gardens, yards, golf courses, forests, and bushes.

They can be found all over North America, from Mexico up to Canada.

Robins eat earth worms, and in the fall and winter they eat lots of berries and fruit.

Robins lay sky blue eggs, three times a year.

Conclusion

We hope you have enjoyed learning about birds found in North America.

If you want to learn more ask your parents to help you log onto the computer or go to your local library.

Download Free Books!

http://MendonCottageBooks.com

Horses For Kids

Amazing Animal Books
For Young Readers
By John and
Annalee Davidson

Ponies For Kids

Mendon Cottage Books

AmazingAnimalBooks
For Young Readers
Rachel Smith

Ten Amazing Horses For Kids

Nature Books for Kids
JD-Biz Publishing
K. Bennett

Akhal-Teke "The Golden Horse of the desert" For Kids

Nature Books for Kids
JD-Biz Publishing
K. Bennett

Suffolk-Punch "The Gentle Giant" For Kids

Nature Books for Kids
JD-Biz Publishing
K. Bennett

Shires "The great Horse" For Kids

Nature Books for Kids
JD-Biz Publishing
K. Bennett

Colonial Spanish "Horse of the Americas" For Kids

Nature Books for Kids
JD-Biz Publishing
K. Bennett

Canadian "The Little Iron Horse" For Kids

Nature Books for Kids
JD-Biz Publishing
K. Bennett

Cleveland Bays "History and Future" Horses For Kids

Nature Books for Kids
JD-Biz Publishing
K. Bennett

Publisher

JD-Biz Corp

P O Box 374

Mendon, Utah 84325

http://www.jd-biz.com/

Download Free Books!

http://MendonCottageBooks.com

www.ingramcontent.com/pod-product-compliance
Lightning Source LLC
Chambersburg PA
CBHW050808290526
45792CB00001B/27